GRIPPED

THE WEIGHT I REFUSED TO CARRY

LOURDES VALTIERRA DIRDEN

EVERYONE HAS A STORY

www.ThinkBooks.org

Copyright © 2025 by
Lourdes Valtierra Dirden

All rights reserved. No part of this book may be reproduced in any form or by any electronic or mechanical means, including information storage and retrieval systems, without written permission from the author, except for the use of brief quotations in a book review.

Edited by Anaiah Davis
Cover by Lourdes Valtierra Dirden
First edition: September 30, 2025

LCCN 2022917207

Print ISBN 978-1-7346592-3-8
Large Print ISBN 978-1-7346592-0-7
Ebook ISBN 978-1-7346592-7-6

These pages were written for those who have lost their way, questioned their place in the world, or carried memories they were afraid to share. Your story is real, and it deserves a voice.

CONTENTS

Introduction	1
1—Footsteps and Shadows	10
2—The Cost of Silence	15
3—Dreams and Nightmares	20
4—Open Wounds	30
5—What The Body Knows	38
6—Meeting Me	52
7—No One Opened The Door	59
8—What Silence Taught Me	66
9—The Inheritance	74
10—Turning The Page	85
Acknowledgments	93
About The Author	95
About The Editor	97
Resources	99

INTRODUCTION

When I was sixty, I found myself packing boxes alone. One by one, I sorted my life into cardboard containers, thunderous voices distracting me as they rang in my ears. The arguments with my husband had become a rhythm I could predict before it even began, a haunting echo that remained long after we stopped speaking. We were separating for the second time, and I no longer recognized myself. I was angry, reactive, then withdrawn, then angry all over again.

I coped by staying busy—working, reading, researching—anything to keep myself moving so I wouldn't have to face what was underneath it all. I didn't know how to fix myself.

When I told my son that I was moving from my childhood friend Marisela's home in Montebello, California, to an apartment in the same city, one located near his grandmother, he offered to help me. We both share a love of writing and the arts, and this has always given us plenty to discuss. Our relationship, particularly in that realm, was built on conversations about the latest books he was reading. His humor and laughter could fill a room, and when he slipped into his playful self, I saw my little boy, which always warmed my heart. I visited his home earlier that week, and I thought moving day might be another opportunity for us to bond. A chance to laugh and work side by side. Instead, it became the day everything shifted.

I rented a U-Haul and waited at the pickup location. When I called and texted

INTRODUCTION

him, he didn't respond. When he finally returned my call, his voice was distant. He said he was on his way.

At the storage unit, my grandson arrived first. Soon after, my son pulled up. He started acting silly, and it made me laugh, but something in his eyes felt far away. We opened the storage door. He stood there, looked at the storage unit, and took a deep breath. "I can't do this," he said.

Without waiting for a response, he turned and walked away. Over his shoulder, he uttered, "When I moved, I paid someone."

"I don't have extra money, Mijo."

"I'll give you money to pay someone," he said, still walking.

I stood there frozen, no breath expelling from my lungs. My grandson, who was around eighteen at the time, came over and hugged me. "It's okay, Grandma. I'll help you."

"Mijo, I know you have to go to work," I said, trying to steady my voice. "Just help me move the refrigerator, and you can go."

He offered to stay again, but I insisted. "It's okay, Mijo. I'll call my brother Carlos. Just help me with the refrigerator, and I'll get help for the rest."

After he left, I called my sister Elva and broke down. She listened quietly, then told me my son had just spoken with her. She explained his reasons for walking away. I listened, numb.

When we hung up, I called Carlos. The moment I heard his voice the tears came again. It startled him. Normally, I'd be angry when I talked about something that upset me, not distressed. When I explained what happened, he told me to pick him up and that he'd try to find someone else to help.

Later that day, my son sent me a text stating that our relationship had been strained for a long time and that I shouldn't contact him. His words landed with a force that left me unsteady. The reason for his withdrawn demeanor at the storage unit wasn't just moving. It was the gravity of everything left unspoken, slowly pulling us apart. That distance had been building for

INTRODUCTION

decades, buried beneath years of unexpressed feelings, neglected needs, and unhealed wounds.

During that time, a sense of dread stayed with me. I feared losing my grandchildren. The tension with my son made me hesitant to reach out, afraid I'd make him angry or put them in the middle. One day, I was part of their lives, and the next, I wasn't.

In April 2024, it had been nearly two-and-a-half years since my son and I had drifted apart. With my granddaughter's fifteenth birthday approaching, she was often on my mind. I sent her a text expressing how much I missed her, how I had been looking through old photos, and how I wanted to hear all about her life now.

Her response brightened my day: *"Hi Grandma, I'm still your granddaughter, don't worry! I'm not sure when, but if you give me a day, I can try to make it happen!"*

Her words showed such wisdom, strength, and maturity beyond her years. I wondered if she sensed the distance between her dad and me, especially since I no longer visited his house. I reminded myself that, as her grandmother, my role wasn't to press her; rather, it was to keep the door open for connecting. Still, the thought of not seeing my grandchildren again lingered like a bitter aftertaste on my tongue.

My son and I would still cross paths at his grandparents' house. We'd hug, exchange polite words, and then part ways. My parents, beaming, would express how good it felt to see us together. I'd nod in agreement while breaking inside. I carried that feeling home every time, smiling on the surface but detonating underneath. He hosted family events I wasn't invited to, even when others in my family were. The shut-out hurt, but the sharper pain was knowing I had helped create the distance between us.

For years, I had been too angry, too reactive, and too consumed by my own battles to notice what my son was carrying—

INTRODUCTION

and part of that burden was me. I didn't know how to reach him, but I did know I needed to face myself. My body had become a vault, holding anger, grief, and silence for decades. If I couldn't rebuild our relationship yet, maybe I could start by understanding what lived inside me.

Awareness didn't arrive gently; it struck like a blunt force, especially after my mom died. Grief didn't come in the way I expected. There was no collapse, no flood of tears. Instead, I clung to the habits that kept me afloat during my separation, anything to keep me from unraveling. It took months before I could walk back into my parents' home. My brothers were caring for our dad, and I was grateful, but I couldn't face or speak to him.

A part of me blamed my dad for my mom's death—not the moment itself, but the years before that wore her down. I held him responsible for how our mom's spirit diminished, how she stopped laughing, abandoning the things she once loved. I knew it wasn't fair, but the anger sat in me like a stone I couldn't dislodge.

Therapy, podcasting, and journaling helped me peel back some of the layers, but a part of me still felt stuck. My mom stayed in a house she worked hard for with a man who never saw her pain. She loved that home, but over time, it became a place stripped bare. He cut down her plants, claimed her space, and chipped away at her peace, piece by piece, until the house that should have sheltered her became more of a prison than a safe haven.

She endured in silence. Sometimes she confided in her daughters, but when we offered to intervene, she'd wave us off, saying, "Ya sabes cómo es. No va a cambiar." ("You know how he is. He's not going to change.")

I refused to be the woman who left this world with a nonexistent voice. I wanted to take the reins of my life, to look clearly at what was before me instead of stumbling down the same well-worn path. If I didn't change, I knew I would end up like her—

INTRODUCTION

trapped and carrying regret to the grave. My life would be different.

Gripped tells the story of how I confronted the fear that used to tighten like a hand around my throat, and the silence that followed. It is the journey of finally laying down what was never mine to carry.

1—FOOTSTEPS AND SHADOWS

You don't know it's fear the first time you experience it. Fear builds in the moments you can't name, the ones that live in your body long before they reach your mind.

Mine began with a sound.

I grew up in a home filled with love and silence, but there were also shadows I didn't yet understand. Much of my early life is blurry, but the sound of a knock at the door has stayed with me for more than fifty years.

My family lived in East Los Angeles, near Roosevelt High School. I was six or seven at the time, and my youngest brother, Ernie, was still a baby. A small Polaroid from

1—FOOTSTEPS AND SHADOWS

those days shows us kids—Ernie in a baby seat, with Lilia, Carlos, Elva, and me crowded close—in the living room. We looked so small, so innocent, not knowing what was coming. I remember the front stairs vividly, not for the steps themselves, but for the way they carried me toward something I didn't yet have words for, a heaviness that rose in my chest each time someone knocked.

The memory always starts the same. There was pounding at the door. My siblings looked at me, their older sister, eyes wide and pleading. Just a child myself, I led them anyway. We ran crying, hiding under the bed or crouching under the kitchen sink while I tried to shield them with my body. I didn't know what we were running from, only that the knock meant danger.

Elva on my lap, Carlos, Lilia, baby is Ernie 1967-1968

My mom once told my Tía Josefina, "No sé por qué estos niños lloran." ("I don't know why these kids cry.") She never explained what was happening. Maybe she understood more than we did, but as children we couldn't have known. She kept everything quiet, as if her silence, and our ignorance, could protect us. In some ways, it did, but it also taught us that silence was a form of survival.

Years later, I asked my brother Carlos if he remembered the knocking at that house with the stairs. He said, casually, "Yeah, it was the ghost." That's what he remembered. But I had no memory of a ghost, only the sound of fists on wood and the way my body braced before it even reached my ears.

Most of my early childhood is a blank memory bank with no key. I've seen pictures of myself at one or two years old, but I have no trace of those moments inside me—no feelings, no fragments of memories. But there's a photo of my siblings and I from a little later, and I remember the house and the knock that took me apart. Even as an adult, a simple rapping on wood could send

1—FOOTSTEPS AND SHADOWS

a current through my body, one sharp enough to stop my breath. I learned to laugh it off, to joke about it, to defend myself in ways that made me seem tough. But deep down I still carried it, embarrassed that something so ordinary could unravel me.

I don't remember how much I loved my father as a little girl, but I know I did because later in life, I remember feeling happy when I saw him. That affection never erased the simultaneous unease I felt in his presence. They lived side by side, bound together in a way a child cannot separate. Love was supposed to bring comfort, but for me it came laced with tension. That contradiction shaped my belief that love could not be trusted, that remaining quiet was the only form of safety, and that dread was normal.

Even now, I don't know what happened after the knocking stopped. I don't know if he checked on us or if we stopped crying. I've asked my siblings, but they don't remember either. Sometimes I wonder if I had asked them years earlier, the memory might have still been there. But I waited too long, and by the time I finally spoke up, their memories had faded. What I do know is that for me, everything began there, with a knock that split love from safety.

2—THE COST OF SILENCE

Fear didn't simply linger behind the front door of my childhood home. It grew, stretching and flexible, accompanying me past the schoolyard gates. During my fourth or fifth-grade year at Santa Isabel School, I'd feel a familiar sense of panic as the end of each day approached. A girl named Cindy and her friends would sometimes wait for me after class, making fun of me, whispering to each other, and laughing just loud enough for me to hear. Since we lived on the same street, it was impossible to avoid her on my walk home.

One day, I finally decided to respond to

their teasing, but afterward they started running toward me. Terrified, I ran too, leaving my younger brother and sister behind in my rush to escape. The journey home involved climbing a steep hill and crossing over the 110 interstate to reach our house. I didn't run for long before they caught up to me near the freeway. I was wearing a skirt when they knocked me down, and I hit the ground hard, injuring my knee. They laughed at me as I cried all the way home. I hated feeling so exposed in front of my siblings—scared, humiliated, unable to protect them.

I came home in tears, my skin scraped and bleeding. My mom—petite, soft-spoken, and fierce when necessary—walked me straight to Cindy's house. Cindy stood behind her mother, both of us crying. I don't remember the words exchanged between our mothers, only that Cindy never bothered me again.

Years later, as a freshman at Sacred Heart of Jesus, I saw Cindy again across from my house on Herbert Street. We recognized each other instantly. When I asked her

2—THE COST OF SILENCE

if she remembered teasing me, she said no. I laughed as if it were nothing, even though my stomach churned, and I told her the story.

Smirking, I mentioned that I wasn't that scared little girl anymore, hoping she would want to see if I was lying. She smiled politely, but I couldn't tell if she recalled that day or not, so I let it go. That was the last time I saw her.

Sacred Heart of Jesus Freshman 1976

But not all my fear at school came from playground cruelty; some of it stemmed from adults I trusted.

When I was between sixth and seventh grade, one of the priests at Santa Isabel would talk and sit close to me. While we spoke, he would put his hand behind my back and tug on my bra strap. It was subtle enough that someone passing by might not notice, but I felt it every time. This behavior made me feel confused, scared, and unsure of what to do. I stayed silent and didn't tell anyone. Years later, two friends confided in me that they had experienced the same thing. They were just as terrified as I had been. Discovering that I wasn't alone didn't erase my shame; instead, it deepened my understanding of how silence protects the wrong people.

Silence didn't just keep me quiet; it also influenced how I carried myself. I learned to perform confidently while concealing my true feelings. My father's competitiveness played a significant role in those performances, but I didn't fully understand this until the last two years of my mother's life. I saw my dad more often than I had in years. He would say, "Te gané" ("I won") or "Me ganaste" ("You won") over trivial matters, like if he arrived at the house first or if I bought something he had intended to get. To him, it was a game, but competition had been ingrained in me for as long as I could remember.

In seventh grade at Santa Isabel, I was taller than most of the boys, and I consistently won at handball, which didn't sit well

2—THE COST OF SILENCE

with some of them. They began calling me Lurch, after the character from *The Addams Family*. While I loved the show, Lurch, the butler who resembled Frankenstein, was unattractive and awkward. My self-esteem was already fragile, and the nickname cut deep. I would curse and laugh, pretending it didn't bother me, but at night, I cried.

By eighth grade, most of the boys had grown taller and started winning more often. The name-calling stopped, but the damage was already done. On the outside, I continued to show up, acting as if none of it affected me. Inside, I carried the pain of feeling small and the pressure to prove myself just to belong. I didn't know it then, but that same ache—the need to be seen and respected—would resurface years later, manifesting itself in situations that would hurt far more than gym class ridicule.

Santa Isabel 8th grade graduation & parents—1975

3—DREAMS AND NIGHTMARES

Some fears came from people, while others emerged entirely from my own mind. When I was twelve or thirteen, sleep began to slip away from me. I would lie awake, my mind spinning with thoughts. I'd close my eyes and imagine outer space, dark and endless, with Earth floating in it. Then I'd think, if Earth weren't there, only space would exist. And if there's only space, then I'm not really here. Panic would grip me until I opened my eyes and picked up a book to read instead. In those moments, I sometimes pictured the face of God in outer space. That vision calmed me for a mo-

3—DREAMS AND NIGHTMARES

ment, but it was not enough to help me sleep.

One night, as I was reading, I overheard my parents talking in the living room. I heard my father say, "No sé por qué no quiero a Lourdes como a los otros." ("I don't know why I don't love Lourdes the way I love the others.") He said it calmly, as if he were just telling her what time it was. My eyes stayed fixed on the page, but I couldn't read a single word. I stood very still and didn't make any noise. When they went to bed, I cried myself to sleep. I carried that sentence with me for years. I didn't tell anyone. I lacked the words to express the shame I felt. It wasn't just that he didn't love me; it was also that I believed I had done something to deserve it—that perhaps there was something unlovable about me. That memory became part of my wiring, and I wouldn't begin to untangle it until much later.

In the same house, when I was about fourteen, I stood up to my father for the first time. It was over our dog, Tiny, a little dachshund, who had bitten my brother Carlos. Furious, my father grabbed a hammer and came for him. Tiny bolted, wedging himself near the back door. Without thinking, I stepped in front, shielding him. Pain shot through my back—my father's fist connected. He told me to move. I didn't. He hit me again.

Something came alive in me that day. I was terrified, but I was more afraid for Tiny than for myself. I stood tall enough to meet my father's eyes. My cheeks were wet as I said, "No lloro porque me duele. Lloro porque te odio, puto." ("I'm not crying because it hurts. I'm crying because I hate you, motherfucker.")

I had never cursed at him before. I expected another blow. Instead, he turned and walked away. That was the moment I decided he would never hit me again. And he didn't. But another man did.

I was about sixteen when I noticed the boy across the street. He had a wide smile and white teeth, and he was tall and thin. His family was large, with five or six sons

3—DREAMS AND NIGHTMARES

total. I didn't know much about boys, except that I liked them. At school, I was shy, too much of a tomboy, never one to dress up like the other girls. I put on a tough exterior, so the boys didn't notice me.

My father must have sensed boys were on my radar, though we never spoke about it. The boy across the street would sometimes walk over and talk to me when I was outside. My father, strict as always, warned him to stay away. My mom once mentioned that someone had been throwing eggs at our house, and I suspected it was the neighbors' boys.

Not long after, we moved to Montebello where my parents bought a house, and I started seeing the boy from across the street.

The nightmare with my father only intensified. One morning, as I walked to the bus stop with my new boyfriend, I saw my father's car approaching. He saw me, and he saw who was beside me. My chest locked. I turned back, breath shallow, knowing I had to face my dad when I got home.

GRIPPED

As soon as I stepped inside the house, it came. My father's voice exploded through the walls. He hurled words that were not my name, words no father should say to a daughter. "Puta. Cabrona. Vete de esta casa. No eres mija." ("Whore. Bitch. Leave this house. You are not my daughter.")

Sobbing, I begged for his mercy. "¿Dónde me voy? No tengo dónde ir." ("Where do I go? I have nowhere to go.")

"No me importa dónde te vayas, puta. Vete de esta casa. Hija de tu chingada madre." ("I don't care where you go, whore. Get out of this house. Son of a bitch.")

I walked away, my vision blurring. At the corner, my boyfriend was waiting. I went to his house, the one across from my old home. His family let me stay, but the next day he told me I couldn't because his brothers weren't comfortable with me there.

That night it rained. I sat at the back door of a clinic on Whittier Boulevard, the cement cold beneath me, rain soaking through my clothes. Anger and shame pressed into me until I felt hollow. I told my-

3—DREAMS AND NIGHTMARES

self I couldn't tell anyone, couldn't let them know how stupid I had been. Hours later, my boyfriend came for me and told me I could stay after all.

I moved back in with him, but one of his brothers told me he had sexual dreams about me. I felt unsafe. They all slept in the same room. My boyfriend didn't start showing how controlling and manipulative he could be until after I moved in. After about two weeks in that house, word must have spread through my family about my whereabouts.

My mom, dad, Tía Josefina, and even a police detective came looking for me there. My mom begged me to come home. My dad stood behind her, silent, and I could see that he was seething. I turned away.

For a few weeks, I bounced between both homes, trapped in a web of shame and confusion. I eventually went back to live with my parents, but by then, my boyfriend's hold on me had tightened.

I don't remember when the hitting started, but I do remember the alleys. Each time we passed one, he'd tell me to pull over, and when I stopped and parked, he would strike my right upper arm repeatedly as if I were a punching bag in a gym. I never cried; I braced. Passing an alley always made me tense, unsure if his fist would become a weapon again.

    One day, he told me I should learn martial arts because he didn't want to hurt me anymore. He said he had learned karate and knew how to use nunchaku. What he didn't know was that I loved Bruce Lee and had once covered my walls with his posters. I took his warning and turned it into something useful. I began training in Kung Fu San Soo in Montebello.

    And then one day, he punched me in the face at my parents' house after I confronted him about something my sister had said. When he got angry and hit me, I knew instantly he was lying. I fell back, but I had learned in class how to fall without hurting myself. I let my body go limp and pretended to pass out. I could hear him crying, panicked, trying to wake me. Inside, I smiled at

3—DREAMS AND NIGHTMARES

self I couldn't tell anyone, couldn't let them know how stupid I had been. Hours later, my boyfriend came for me and told me I could stay after all.

I moved back in with him, but one of his brothers told me he had sexual dreams about me. I felt unsafe. They all slept in the same room. My boyfriend didn't start showing how controlling and manipulative he could be until after I moved in. After about two weeks in that house, word must have spread through my family about my whereabouts.

My mom, dad, Tía Josefina, and even a police detective came looking for me there. My mom begged me to come home. My dad stood behind her, silent, and I could see that he was seething. I turned away.

For a few weeks, I bounced between both homes, trapped in a web of shame and confusion. I eventually went back to live with my parents, but by then, my boyfriend's hold on me had tightened.

I don't remember when the hitting started, but I do remember the alleys. Each time we passed one, he'd tell me to pull over, and when I stopped and parked, he would strike my right upper arm repeatedly as if I were a punching bag in a gym. I never cried; I braced. Passing an alley always made me tense, unsure if his fist would become a weapon again.

One day, he told me I should learn martial arts because he didn't want to hurt me anymore. He said he had learned karate and knew how to use nunchaku. What he didn't know was that I loved Bruce Lee and had once covered my walls with his posters. I took his warning and turned it into something useful. I began training in Kung Fu San Soo in Montebello.

And then one day, he punched me in the face at my parents' house after I confronted him about something my sister had said. When he got angry and hit me, I knew instantly he was lying. I fell back, but I had learned in class how to fall without hurting myself. I let my body go limp and pretended to pass out. I could hear him crying, panicked, trying to wake me. Inside, I smiled at

3—DREAMS AND NIGHTMARES

his whimpers, and I knew then I had to leave him.

Martial arts gave me the opening I needed to learn self-defense. I threw myself into training, eager to practice with higher belts. I wanted to know how to respond if someone grabbed me from behind, yanked my hair, pressed their hand against my throat, or swung for my face. I didn't shy away from bigger opponents; I welcomed them. The bigger they were, the better. I wanted to be ready for anything.

But there was a fury in me, and it showed. My instructor told me I needed to learn how to relax. He said he could see it when I trained—how easily I could hurt someone, even in practice. Being a lower belt didn't change that. What he saw was the anger that rose in me the moment it was my turn to defend myself.

When my boyfriend came to watch me train, my instructor, Al Hinojosa, would meet his gaze and push him out of the room without a word. Al became one of my first mentors. Learning Kung Fu San Soo didn't just give me confidence to leave; it also proved I could protect myself.

The arm punching stopped. Eventually, I ended it. We had been together for about two years. Looking back, I see martial arts as more than defense. It proved that I could build strength where I had once only known fear. I started to learn what it felt like to finally stand my ground.

But the newfound strength in my body didn't settle what stirred inside me mentally and emotionally. Around the age of seventeen, I started having panic attacks, though I didn't know that's what they were called at the time. My chest would lock tight, my breath would hitch in my throat, the room would tilt. I needed help, but I neither asked for it, nor was it offered. Instead, I pressed on. I graduated high school with honors, although my late transfer prevented me from reaching the highest distinction. I enrolled at California State University, Los Angeles, with English as my major.

One professor, after seeing my high school record, offered me a chance to re-

3—DREAMS AND NIGHTMARES

take a midterm because I scored low. I let it pass, not because I lacked ability, but because I was carrying too much. My home life was turbulent, and I was still entangled in the shadow of my first boyfriend, who wouldn't let go. I didn't yet know how to handle that kind of pressure, and the confusion kept me from moving forward. I quit school.

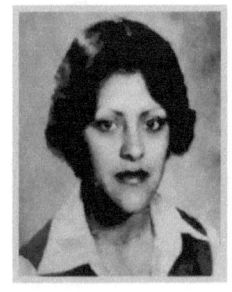

Montebello High School Senior 1979

4—OPEN WOUNDS

My son's father was my second boyfriend. I met him in April 1982, just after I turned twenty-one. I was celebrating my birthday with my first margarita at a Mexican restaurant in Los Angeles, off Soto Street and Olympic Boulevard, that featured live music. I came to the celebration with a friend who was a few years older.

    My son's father was at the restaurant with his older brother, and I later discovered that he would turn eighteen in November. He looked much older than seventeen, and I will never forget the day he came to see me, nervously handing me a card that said,

4—OPEN WOUNDS

"Roosevelt High School ROTC." I was shocked to realize that I was dating someone who was still in high school.

We hadn't been dating for very long before I discovered I was pregnant. I had been so naïve—I didn't realize that missing my period for a few months could mean I was expecting. After taking a urine test, I found out that I was about four-and-a-half months along. We were both young, and he was even younger than I was. I was terrified. Initially, I didn't view having a child as a positive thing because I truly believed I wouldn't be a good mother.

I was twenty-two when I had my son in August 1983. The moment he was placed on my chest for the first time, his tiny body was warm against mine, fists curling tightly as I listened to the gentle rhythm of his breaths. I studied him, noting the dimples beginning to show on his cheeks, the way his eyes seemed to take me in. Love rose up in me—fierce, immediate, undeniable. I held him, and a question edged its way in. Could I give him what he needed? The moment carried both wonder and unease, setting the stage for what lay ahead.

We informed my parents about the pregnancy, and he also let his mother know. Shortly after, we took a spontaneous trip to Las Vegas and got married. At that time, I was already working at the police department, having started my career at the age of twenty-one. We rented a house in Montebello, where his mother lived with us and became our babysitter. She adored her grandson.

We were together for about two-and-a-half years when we split, and for roughly half of that time, we were married. At that time, I was young and didn't fully understand the meaning of family. I loved my son and wanted him with me, but my perception of family had been distorted long before, and my priorities were misaligned. His father and I tried to reconcile several times until our son was about four years old.

Love, in my world, had always been entangled with fear. Even when I wanted to feel safe, I didn't know how. Every man I dated felt like he could be "the one," but none ever were. While I didn't let anyone control me, I was limited by my own mindset. I thought I knew what was best for me, but I didn't. I was filled with anger I couldn't comprehend, and I didn't realize the extent of the damage done to my mind during childhood.

My distorted perception of love became evident in the unfulfilling relationships I experienced, which I mistakenly equated with love at the time. I often believed that being intimate with someone I was dating meant I was in love; however, that was not true. The excitement I felt when meeting someone new, hoping he might be "the one," ultimately led to disappointment.

Why did this happen? I did not love, value, or respect myself. My constant pursuit of control only added to my struggles.

Many of the arguments I experienced in those relationships were senseless, but I couldn't recognize that then. I built up walls, always prepared for confrontation. Growing up in an unstable environment filled with pointless conflict, especially initiated by my father, shaped me. My mother tried to make sense of a man who only understood chaos, doing her best to defend herself and her children.

Born in Texas, my father was the youngest child in his family and was abandoned by his dad when he was around two years old. Shortly after, his mother passed away, and he was sent to live with family friends in Mexico, where he was treated like Cinderella—the unwanted stepchild. The narrative never changed when my dad recounted it. He was beaten with whips and once struck on the head with the lady of the house's high-heeled shoe. As a young boy, he had to work just to get food. He endured this harsh life until his siblings found him when he was about seventeen and brought him back to Texas. Without knowing how to heal from such profound suffering, it was

Dad in front of his home—2025

nearly impossible for my father's trauma not to impact his wife and children.

Ultimately, the love I sought in my relationships proved to be a waste of time. I found myself lost in my own thoughts, still searching for the affection of my father, who didn't love me in the way I needed him to. He had always wanted his firstborn to be a son but got me instead. In this aspect of my life, I was not a good mother to my son.

Dad and me 2010

I remember a couple of instances where I was forced to use my martial arts skills. In one relationship, my partner, who was a little over six feet tall, had a habit of occasionally pushing me. I didn't make a big deal out of it at first. I still tended not to express my true feelings, often masking them with laughter, even when there was something more serious underneath. He would laugh too, likely considering it a joke.

One day, while we were at the market, I

had finally had enough. I suddenly grabbed his wrist and put it in a lock, causing him to fall slightly to the ground. It was a move designed to control his wrist. I told him I was tired of his behavior and asked him to stop. He agreed, and I let him go. After that day, he never pushed me again.

On another occasion, another man in my life became upset and grabbed me by the arm. I didn't give him a chance to do anything further. I quickly turned around, pushed him away, and he nearly fell backward. I yelled some profanities, and he backed off. Unsure if he was going to attack me, my instinct was to defend myself.

None of that erased the deeper truth. I was raising a son while still trying to grow up myself. My anger, confusion, and search for love all spilled into the world he was growing up in. I wanted to protect him, yet I often introduced men into his life who should never have been there. That contradiction defined my early years as a mother.

I wasn't the mother I aspired to be at that time. I loved my son deeply, but I was

4—OPEN WOUNDS

still struggling with my own wounds, many of which I didn't fully realize existed until later in life. It took me years to understand that being a mother wasn't just about caring for him. It was also about learning to care for myself.

5—WHAT THE BODY KNOWS

I met my husband over a pool table in February 2011, just days before Valentine's Day. Our conversation had turned to the holiday when I mentioned that I didn't like crowds, and he felt the same. That small agreement created a sense of common ground between us.

That night, I set a quarter on the edge of the pool table to mark my turn. A little later, he walked over, handed me the coin, and asked if I was ready to play. One game turned into several. No one else put up their quarters, so it was just the two of us, trading shots as the drinks eased our

5—WHAT THE BODY KNOWS

guards. Our words carried a teasing edge, laughter spilling over as we tossed playful remarks back and forth as easily as the pool balls rolled across the table. His smile lit up the room, and his deep, calm voice drew me in.

We exchanged phone numbers, and when I suggested he call me on Valentine's Day instead of going out, he did. We spent that evening talking and laughing, and before long, we had made plans to see each other again.

As we got to know each other better, we discovered how well we complemented one another. Our shared perspectives, ambitions, and approaches to work aligned, creating a strong bond between us. We spent more than four years together before marrying in November 2015, when I was fifty-four.

Early in our relationship, we'd slip into the car for long road trips. With the windows down and the horizon stretching wide, we realized how much we both enjoyed being on the open road, ready for whatever adventures came our way. We loved going to the movies, sometimes attending plays, and often returning to the stories that connected us. His is tucked away, and mine is still unfolding on the page. Writing became part of our rhythm as he read my drafts and helped me smooth out the edges.

Our chemistry stemmed from both our differences and similarities. He brought a quiet steadiness to life, while I carried a fierce passion. His presence didn't extinguish my flame; it gave it direction, allowing it to burn brighter without consuming me.

Eventually, I stopped drinking. Alcohol never mixed well with my anger or the traumas I hadn't faced. Although I could still enjoy a drink or two, I decided to leave it behind. Before I met my husband, I sometimes went to a bar alone, carrying a notebook like others might carry a shield. I'd sip a drink and let my words settle me.

One evening, a man across the bar called out, "Hey, beautiful, what are you writing?" At first, I ignored him. He spoke louder.

5—WHAT THE BODY KNOWS

I looked up, smiled, and answered politely, "It's just a story." When he pressed again, I said, "Do you mind? I just want to write."

His response was sharp and loud: "You're at a fuckin' bar. Why are you acting like a bitch?"

There were only a few people around, but I still felt heat rush to my face, with anger and embarrassment rising in equal measure. The bartender leaned in to address him, though I couldn't hear what she said. I didn't respond. Instead, I closed the story I'd been working on and wrote down our exchange. The insult lost its sting once it hit the page. Writing has always provided me with a way to set down my pain.

In March 2019, I was fifty-seven, and my husband and I separated for the first time. My son helped me move my belongings into storage and invited me to stay with him and his family. For a while, I lived with them, enjoying the company of my youngest grandchildren every day. The change of scenery and love from my family brought me a sense of peace. By May of that same year, I had moved into an apartment near my job.

Even before that decision, I had started seeking help in a different way. For years, I had focused all my energy on my mind and spirit while unintentionally ignoring my body. I just kept myself busy, telling myself I'd come back to it.

In January 2019, I wrote a long email to Robert, a former YMCA trainer I had worked with fourteen years earlier. By then, I had survived a car accident, gone through physical therapy, and carried family stress that felt like gravel grinding in my shoes—small, constant, and unrelenting. I wanted to move forward, but my body had stopped cooperating. I wasn't just frustrated by the weight gain and knee pain; I was frustrated with myself. It felt like I had betrayed my own efforts yet again.

In that email, I poured everything out. My writing. The podcast I wanted to build. The car accident in August 2018. The pain that clung to me. The excuses I stacked like sandbags. I ended with a single, stripped-down question: "Where do I start?"

Three months before his reply arrived. When it did, he met me point by point, addressing the doubts I had spilled onto the screen. He caught me up on his own life—he was now married—and laid out a plan that was clear, practical, and demanding. He didn't speak as though I was broken. He didn't pad his words. Instead, he reminded me of the strength he had once seen in me and outlined a way back.

Robert had been more than a trainer. He was a mentor. Though a few years younger than my son, he carried himself with a discipline that seemed older than his age: balancing college and work, speaking with unshakable clarity, and pushing himself forward with quiet resolve. In many ways, he mirrored my son—focused, determined, tenacious.

"BENCH. SQUAT. DEADLIFT," he wrote. "Powerlifting is a great community. Focusing on just three exercises makes balancing mind, spirit, and body much easier."

I read those words repeatedly. They weren't just about exercise. They felt like blueprints, providing a structure where I had previously seen only collapse. Each line seemed less like mere instruction and more like a handhold—something solid to hold onto when everything else felt unsteady. It was a way to reconnect with my own body again.

Then came his blunt reminder, as sharp as a slap: "Bust your ass. Don't sweat anything else."

After I lost momentum and began to wonder if change was still possible, those words gave me direction. One lift. One rep. One honest day at a time. I didn't jump in immediately—my knees throbbed, and my mom's health was beginning to decline. Life pulled me sideways again. But even without training, his words hummed through me like a persistent current. Robert didn't see me for what I lacked. He saw the vision of what I could still become.

I started researching others who had walked this path and found Tammy White,

5—WHAT THE BODY KNOWS

Ernestine Shepherd, Dave Durell, and Susan Niebergall. Susan drew me in most—she was a powerlifter—and Dave, too, because he was over sixty and carried the credibility of decades as a trainer and physical therapist.

Eventually, I chose Susan for training, but I continued to follow Dave. I joined Susan's Inner Circle on Facebook and read her posts on Instagram. Each day, someone shared a question, a setback, or a victory, and someone else always answered. There were workouts for every level, with and without weights, alongside advice for beginners. I wasn't sure what to expect, but I knew I had stepped into a community where learning and encouragement were passed hand to hand like a torch.

All the while, my body reminded me of its limits. My right knee ached with arthritis, and my left—still marked by the accident in 2018—joined in its protest.

In August 2022, I was sixty-one, and at first, I could barely manage a deadlift. The moment I tried, I felt the warning tug of a muscle ready to give, so I leaned on alternatives—dumbbell programs, long warm-ups—anything that would build strength without breaking me. I worked my way up slowly, preparing myself for the 90-Day Challenge. Even so, the thought of exercise on the floor terrified me. I imagined myself stuck there, unable to rise. Lunges were another battle. My right knee locked me out, refusing to bend to my will.

By October, I began The Unicorn 90-Day Fat Loss Challenge, a program designed to help you burn fat and build strength. The first few weeks were brutal. In that opening week, I couldn't even finish the sets. Some days, pain blurred my eyes with tears, the weight of frustration as heavy as any barbell. I skipped squats, avoided the floor, and left the barbell bare, unable to load it with weight. But I refused to quit.

By the time I finished the challenge in the second week of December, I could manage step-ups, balance through floor work with a physio ball, and—best of all—deadlift. I worked my way up to fifty-six

5—WHAT THE BODY KNOWS

pounds, a number that felt monumental after my initial struggle. Today, I can lift over one hundred pounds.

That group became more than just a workout space; it was a form of medicine. Women and men in their fifties, sixties, and seventies cheered each other on like teammates in a race we were all still running. We weren't only celebrating heavier lifts or smaller waistlines. We were celebrating quiet victories: showing up after a punishing week, honoring the days our bodies needed rest, and learning that progress wasn't about driving ourselves into the ground; it was about listening, and lifting again tomorrow.

One day, a new member named Michele introduced herself in a post. She was sixty-five, newly retired from nursing, and she hoped the group would help her succeed. Her words stopped me cold. I saw myself reflected there. The same doubts I once carried: *Can I really do this? Am I too late? What if my body gives out?*

So, I replied. I told her what I had gone

through and that I was sixty-one when I started, that it got easier, but not right away.

"YOU will succeed," I wrote.

Michele wrote back to say my message helped her believe she could keep going. Her words felt like a hand extended through the screen. That small exchange—just a few sentences between strangers—moved me, because sometimes, the most powerful thing we can do is remind someone that they're not alone.

In the quiet moments after my move, I turned to writing and sometimes recorded my thoughts during long commutes. I wasn't entirely sure why I did it, but it loosened something in me, like steam releasing from a covered pot. When I listened back, I could hear the truth I had been trying to outrun, the hollow ache that had been pressing against my chest. I sought out motivational speakers, not to escape but to borrow their words when mine refused to form. I listened to Marisa Peer, Jim Kwik, Louise Hay, Don Miguel Ruiz, his sons, and his niece, Karla Ruiz. I read Gloria Steinem and John

5—WHAT THE BODY KNOWS

Bradshaw. Their voices gave shape to what I had carried silently, their messages clearer than anything I could yet name on my own.

Still, restlessness stirred, and an old question pressed at me again and again: whose hand had been behind that knock? In 2018 or 2019, I had lunch with Marisela, who lived with us in the house with the stairs when she was about eleven or twelve. Her grandmother, Silve, had helped care for us back then. Over plates of food, I admitted that the sound of knocking still unsettled me, how I sometimes dropped my voice low, roughening it to sound stronger than I felt, as though a tone could keep danger on the other side of the door. I even laughed while telling her how I once startled my niece, barking out, "Who is it?" only to hear her reply, "Tía, it's just me. You scared me."

Elva front, Carlos, Lilia, Me, Marisela 1967-1968

When I mentioned how my siblings and I

used to hide, Marisela paused before saying, "That was your dad knocking."

I froze. "My dad?"

"Yes. He used to come home drunk and knock on the door. You and your brothers and sisters would run and hide under the bed."

The realization struck harder than all the years I'd tried to bury it. For over five decades, that sound had haunted me, tied to the memories I had locked away: my father was unpredictable and volatile when he drank.

I feared him more than I loved him, and this contradiction carved its own scar. Love should have felt like shelter, but with my father, it carried the weight of dread. I remembered no warmth in his arms, only the thud of fists against the door and the way terror jolted through me each time. The body remembers what the mind tries to shut out.

As a result, I carried pieces of my father's shadow into my marriage. My husband and I were apart for nine months, living separate lives until his layoff pulled us

5—WHAT THE BODY KNOWS

back into the same orbit. We decided to try again and moved back in together. But the cycle eventually repeated itself—arguments circled like vultures, silence thickened between us, and soon it was as though no time had passed at all.

When I turned sixty, I could no longer hide behind the illusion that this was something done to me. The cycle wasn't forced on me —I had stepped back into it with my own feet. My mom's declining health became the excuse I clung to, the curtain I pulled around choices I didn't want to face. Once more, I separated from my husband and moved in with Marisela to be closer to my mom. For two months, her home became a kind of waiting room, a pause between what I was leaving behind and the place I would eventually claim as my own.

Marisela left, Me, Lilia—2018

6—MEETING ME

When the noise of my life finally fell away, I felt like I was drowning. Everything around me was still, yet underneath the silence something stirred: my voice. It was faint and unfamiliar, almost like hearing a stranger call from a distance, but it was mine.

For most of my life, I had lived in reaction. I was the one easing tense situations, patching problems, keeping myself moving so no one else would come undone. Without those constant demands, I no longer knew who I was. I had been so accustomed to bending and making myself small that standing still felt foreign.

6—MEETING ME

I had been alone before and enjoyed it, filling hours with my work, research, writing, and podcast prep. But this time was different. This wasn't peace; it was emptiness, a hollow tree where a sense of self should have been, thick and strong.

On the outside, I appeared functional. Inside, I was unraveling—tired, ashamed, and weighed down by confusion. I did everything I could to hold the seams together so no one else would see.

After the second separation from my husband, I turned inward again, but with a different kind of awareness. It wasn't just that I had been wounded in the marriage; I had also caused harm. Without respect for myself, I could not truly offer him respect either. I was reactive and angry, blinded by my own unhealed traumas.

That second separation, tangled with the grief of estrangement from my son, forced me into a reckoning. I felt embarrassed, ashamed that as an older adult, I still hadn't figured it out. At the time, it didn't feel like healing—it felt like falling apart. But beneath the rubble, something essential was waiting to be uncovered: me.

My sisters and Marisela became anchors for me, giving me ground when everything else felt unsteady. Elva urged me to consider who I was without anyone's opinion, without the constant need to prove myself. I didn't have an answer then, but her question quietly planted itself and grew roots in my brain.

When my mom was dying, she sometimes asked if my son and I were talking again. Some days, I told her yes. Other days, I told her the truth and watched the pain settle in her eyes. Family was everything to my mom. She couldn't understand how a child could walk away. I didn't know how to explain it in a way that wouldn't hurt her.

When the estrangement began, I told both my parents, and I saw the sorrow cross their faces. They couldn't mend it, and neither could I. I carried the weight of failure, as if I had broken something sacred.

I threw myself into work and self-improvement, building my website, reading endlessly, tumbling down YouTube and TED Talk rabbit holes of motivational voices.

During my commutes, the recordings I had begun years earlier became something different. This time, I spoke aloud as though I were both confessor and witness, naming old memories, questioning beliefs, saying the words I had swallowed for decades.

Playing them back became a catalyst. I heard the despondence, exhaustion, and even sometimes amusement in my voice, but I also recognized flashes of clarity. Writing had helped me before, but speaking out loud was rawer, impossible to soften or disguise.

There are countless teachers, experts, and guides, but their words don't matter until you're ready to hear them. For me, two voices finally cut through the static: Marisa Peer and Jim Kwik.

Seeing Peer's "I Am Enough" movement felt like a veil being lifted from my eyes. For decades, I had lived by the belief that I was not enough, measured against my father's anger, my family's silence, my role as protector, and my mistakes as a mother. Each failure reinforced the lie that something in me was missing. Her words didn't erase that history, but they revealed how much of my life had been built on a false foundation.

Kwik's story and his relentless determination to learn and rebuild his mind reminded me that I had always been capable of change. I wasn't lost; I had only been looking at myself through the lens of shadows and silence. His message pressed me to remember the woman who had endured, created, raised a son, and kept moving even when she wanted to collapse. For years, I measured myself by what I lacked. His reminder pushed me to name what had always been mine: resilience, creativity, and persistence.

Those lessons gave me the strength to take the next step. I reached out to Elizabeth Valdez, a hypnotherapist who was trained by Peer, and she listened without judgment and crafted a recording for me to play each night. Her voice became the one I

6—MEETING ME

fell asleep to. But it wasn't only the recording that helped. When I returned a few weeks later, she walked me through the changes—some so small I might have overlooked them on my own. I was speaking more gently to myself, noticing moments of gratitude, feeling that my shoulders weren't up near my ears as often. She reminded me of the parts of myself I had buried, the strength I kept forgetting was mine.

Change wasn't sudden. It came in increments, the way light seeps in through a half-closed curtain. Slowly, space—a breath, a pause—appeared between the sting of a trigger and my reaction. That pause became the ground I could stand on.

Therapy had once opened doors for me, but this time I didn't just glance inside; I crossed the threshold. I began showing up for myself in small but steady rituals, scribbling down words that stayed with me, not to memorize them, but to sketch the contours of who I was becoming.

Over time, I saw that I was no longer moving through life on autopilot, clinging to

GRIPPED

survival. I had met myself at last—not the version muffled by fear or shaped to fit other people's frames—but the one waiting behind the locked door, patient and persistent, wanting only to be seen and heard.

7—NO ONE OPENED THE DOOR

because I had an insatiable need to know more.

Reflecting on my past, I often consider the source of that desire to learn. Although I didn't realize it at the time, my mom had a deep love for reading about distant lands, biographies, history, and geography. While she may not have assisted me with my homework, she provided me with something even more valuable: a sense of curiosity. Her books opened doors to knowledge that she couldn't personally explore, and without knowing it, she handed me the keys to those worlds.

That curiosity followed me into adulthood. Over the years, I worked in administrative, investigative, and creative roles. I wrote and self-published *Going Solar: The Homeowner's Handbook*. I built my author website and created a publishing imprint, Think Books. I even produced and hosted a podcast. Looking at it all together felt like spreading puzzle pieces across a table and realizing that, without knowing it, I'd been assembling a picture all along.

In June 2023, I launched VA 4 Solutions, a virtual assistance business. My foundation rested on years of experience working for others—managing projects, streamlining processes, and smoothing the flow of daily operations. Now, instead of building someone else's vision, I support authors, writers, podcasters, and business owners with content management, self-publishing, business systems, and design—anything that keeps their work on track.

Starting a business was both thrilling and lonely. I craved connection with others who understood the challenge of carving out something on your own. That October, I joined the Introvert VA Club, created by Billie Gardner of the *Desire to Done* podcast. After discovering her voice, her words struck something in me. That community took me in like kin, offering tools, ideas, and confidence I hadn't realized I was lacking.

Not long after my layoff, I unearthed old journals and short stories. They weren't just words on a page; they were snapshots of a younger me, fragments I had never spoken

7—NO ONE OPENED THE DOOR

aloud but had carried with me. They revealed the patterns I hadn't recognized before—the trauma, the learned behaviors, the way my past had threaded itself through every chapter of my life.

Soon after, I launched my podcast and author newsletter and recommitted to finishing this memoir. Losing my job didn't just push me into self-employment; it ignited a fire. My business, my podcast, and my writing are not simply projects. They are proof that I no longer wait for someone else's permission to step forward.

8—WHAT SILENCE TAUGHT ME

I never imagined my voice would travel beyond the walls of my own home, let alone find its way to strangers. For much of my life, what I said was trimmed and tamed by fear, shaped by what I thought was safe to say. I grew up believing emotions were dangerous territory. No one told us not to cry, but we learned by watching. When feelings spilled over in front of my father, the air turned brittle. If he was drinking, each step across the room felt like walking barefoot on glass. We—my mom included—made ourselves smaller, quieter, careful not to trigger whatever was already brewing.

8—WHAT SILENCE TAUGHT ME

As I got older, I didn't know how to give shape to what lived inside me. I yelled when I was angry, but my words were a wall, not a bridge. Sarcasm became my shield, deflecting the truths I couldn't bring myself to name. I could make people laugh, but it was just the mask for what I wouldn't reveal. The moment I felt exposed, I either went silent or armed myself, ready for a battle that might not come. Living that way made the world feel like a battlefield, even in moments that should have been safe.

When my son stopped speaking to me and my mom's health began to decline, I could no longer sidestep what was pressing at me. The shape of my days demanded attention—how I was living, what I believed, how I reacted, and how I avoided. I didn't want to face those emotions, but they settled in quietly and refused to leave. I was frustrated, sad, and tired of pacing the same loop with no way out.

Instead of dodging, I began tracing the lines of where I came from—my father's sudden bursts of rage, my mom's silences that swallowed the air in whole rooms, the fear that etched itself into me, and the disappointments I stacked away like boxes in a closet. Whether I meant to or not, I knew parts of that history had seeped into the lives of those around me.

So I dug. I journaled, not just to keep a record, but also to pull apart the knots I had avoided for too long. Even as I searched for ways to mend, a part of me resisted. I knew the hardest barrier was myself. Still, I read, I learned, and I refused to lay the work down. One book that steadied me was John Bradshaw's *Healing the Shame that Binds You.* It gave shape and names to feelings I had never been able to articulate.

Dr. Gabor Maté's work met me quietly but powerfully. His writing on trauma, addiction, and childhood development helped me recognize what I had long felt but never fully understood. *In the Realm of Hungry Ghosts* and his talks online opened windows where I had seen only walls. Through his lens, my father's rage began to make more sense. I could finally see how my mother's silence had settled into me like a blueprint, shaping the way I learned to hold back my voice.

By then, I had been recording my thoughts for months. It was less about unraveling the past and more about watching myself take shape in the present. Those recordings made me wonder how many other women were doing the same, speaking into the quiet, trying to make sense of what they had carried. I wanted to build something where another woman could hear even a fragment of recognition and feel less alone.

I had been listening to podcasts for years, so I began studying how to create one of my own. Tutorials, articles, equipment guides—I pieced it together step by step. What I knew for certain was that I wanted to reach older adults, especially women searching for answers and holding on to themselves through it all.

I also began researching aging and community resources, reading through materials from the California Department of Aging and exploring Los Angeles County services. Still, one question pressed louder than the rest: What did older adults like me truly want to hear? The answer became the ground on which my podcast was built.

Around the same time, I joined a three-day online class for women focused on personal growth and self-expression. That's where I met Teresa—a stranger then, now a friend and collaborator.

During our first Zoom call, the instructor asked us to share something personal. Teresa spoke, her voice steady but raw, and it was clear her words were coming from a deep place. But halfway through, she was interrupted and gently redirected. I felt a wave rise in me—first confusion, then anger.

When someone is just beginning to let their voice out, even a soft interruption can feel like another reminder to stay quiet. I knew that silence in my bones. I couldn't stop thinking about it. I wanted to tell her, *"I'll listen."*

So I searched for her on LinkedIn, and to my surprise, she had already been looking for me. We connected first online,

8 — WHAT SILENCE TAUGHT ME

then by phone, and slowly built a friendship. What began as a moment of solidarity turned into an ongoing exchange—two women choosing not to carry everything alone.

At the time, I had been practicing how to pause before reacting, trying not to let anger or hurt lead the way. What happened to Teresa struck a chord I knew well. The frustration of not being able to give voice to what sits inside you. Her experience reflected so many of my own, which is why it left such a mark.

The instructor had a plan, a structure she wanted to follow, but in that instant, it felt like the human part of the exchange was lost. Still, I could see myself in her, too. I thought of the times I had redirected or interrupted someone else, not out of disregard, but because discomfort or uncertainty pushed me there. It was a reminder that all of us are still learning how to leave room for others, and for ourselves.

February 5, 2024, I launched *Growing Older Together*, the day after my mom's ninety-fifth birthday. My first season unfolded in sixteen episodes, with titles like "When the Past Knocks," "Echoes of Resilience," and "Unresolved Emotions." Season two added nine more before I paused in December 2024 as my mom's health declined. By then, I had built something I loved. A place where my voice could travel farther than I ever imagined, carrying honesty, stories, and resources into the airwaves, with the hope that someone might feel less alone.

Podcast mic 2024

Speaking into the mic never unsettled me. I liked hearing my voice. Sometimes listeners sent messages: *"Thank you for talking about what I've been feeling," "I love your podcast,"* or simply, *"You have a soothing voice."* Even a single thumbs-up or heart landed with weight. Those small signs reminded me that impact isn't measured in

8—WHAT SILENCE TAUGHT ME

numbers. One voice reaching one heart was enough.

Podcasting didn't just connect me with others—it reconnected me to myself. It softened the way I spoke with my family and with my husband. Our marriage has carried its share of silence, frustration, and distance. We've stepped apart more than once, but somehow, we've always circled back. He tends to his work, I tend to mine, and still, we meet in the middle. Our story isn't seamless, but it's stitched together by choice, and for that, I'm grateful.

Each episode taught me more than how to lean into a microphone. It reminded me where my voice was born—in the years of holding it back, in the cracks where truth yearned to be heard. Now, after so many years of silence, I send my words into the world like signals across the dark, trusting they'll find who needs them.

9—THE INHERITANCE

My mom passed away on March 17, 2025. Her death pulled open a door I had kept shut, forcing me to face complicated emotions. Her body had been failing for years, but her spirit carried wounds just as painful. Not long after, I confided in a relative, the words spilling out before I could catch them: *"I feel like my father killed her."* The sentence startled me, but in that moment, it captured the truth of my feelings.

    At first, I thought all my anger was aimed at my father. But as the days stretched on, I realized part of it reached to-

9—THE INHERITANCE

ward my mother as well. Even in death, I was still trying to guard her from him, as if the old patterns had outlived her. She was gone, and yet I remained in the middle, resenting the choices that had kept her tethered to a life bound by fear and obligation. I know she hadn't made those choices to harm us, but they harmed her just the same. She loved her children fiercely and gave what she could with the tools she had.

My parents' marriage was never peaceful. To the outside world, it might have looked ordinary, but inside those walls, the truth was unavoidable. Even after my father stopped drinking in his late forties, the storms didn't end; they changed form. The bottle disappeared, but his voice still cracked through the house like thunder. Control hung thick in the air, and his moods shifted without warning. Only later did I see how some of those same patterns had taken root in me.

By December 2024, my mom was fading quickly. Her will to live remained strong, but her body was giving out. She struggled with multiple illnesses, and by the end, she couldn't walk or see the garden she once loved. My siblings and I took turns caring for her. Every night before I went home, I would kiss her forehead and say, "I'll see you tomorrow, Mom." She would respond softly, "Okay, Mija."

Just months earlier, during the summer of that year, she was still getting out with us, using her walker. She joined us at the park, and we circled around her like children again. My sister-in-law, Lisa, was always there with us. My mom's face lit up when she saw her. We sat in the shade, telling stories, our laughter rising into the warm air. And then came a smile that seemed to set her free, if only for a moment. We took pictures because she wanted something she could hold onto, evidence that we were together. A reminder that the

Carlos right, Me behind mom, Lilia left of mom, Ernie, Elva—2024

9—THE INHERITANCE

family she had worked so hard for was still gathered around her.

Those afternoons became small gifts, brief windows where joy broke through. Not long after, her strength faded, and by winter she was bedridden. The house grew quieter, but I carried the sound of her laughter at the park with me, a lantern in the darker months that followed.

By December, evenings were marked by their own rituals. Around seven p.m., she'd start checking the time and say, "Ya vete a descansar." ("Go home and rest.") I'd hold her hand and reply, "Trabajo aquí o en la casa. Así que es mejor estar aquí contigo, ama." ("I'm working here or at home, so it's better to be here with you, Mom.") And I meant it. If I were going to work, I wanted to do it beside her. I was afraid to leave her alone.

We left three small night lights on for her each evening, soft pools of light against the dark. Before leaving, I tucked the blanket around her shoulders to keep her warm and adjusted her position, making sure she was at ease and that my sister Elva could see her clearly on the cameras.

Watching her decline uncovered wounds in me I hadn't realized were still open. As her body gave way, I began to see more clearly the burdens she had shouldered all her life. She lived in the house she helped build, yet those same walls suffocated her. The garden she once tended with joy grew barren. My father cut down the trees, one limb at a time, until even the branches that had once sheltered her were gone. His anger clung to the rooms like damp air. She never said she hated him; she only commented on how he spoke. She'd shrug and say, "Ya sabes cómo es, ignóralo." ("You know how he is, ignore him.")

That resignation wasn't new. It had been her answer for years. Long before her final decline, when we asked if she wanted to leave him, her response was firm: "Yo trabajé para pagar por esta casa y es para mis hijos. Si lo divorcio, tu papá agarraría medio de esta casa, no." ("I worked to pay for this house, and it's for my children. Divorcing

9—THE INHERITANCE

him so your dad can get half of this house, no.") That house was her proof of sacrifice and also her prison. She stayed because she couldn't imagine another way. She believed survival required endurance, and for years, I confused that endurance with love.

In her final months, I witnessed the toll that silence had taken on her. She lacked the tools for processing grief and healing. The year before, I suggested audiobooks, knowing how much she loved to read but could no longer see well. She refused. She didn't want to change or confront anything foreign. She chose the familiarity of silence, even when it left her feeling more isolated. That was the price she paid. I carry that awareness with me now, and it still brings me despair.

I've made peace with much of my sorrow, and my mother still lives in me through her story. For years, I wrote about her—short reflections, recorded conversations, even a draft of a screenplay from a UCLA course. That script still waits in a drawer, but I know it's time to take it out again.

Writing is the thread that keeps me tethered to her, not to reopen the wound, but to keep her truth from fading.

In the weeks before she died, the rhythm of our nights shifted. Before I left, she would whisper "Thank you," and I'd lean down to kiss her forehead, answering softly, "You're welcome, Mom." I often walked away with tears blurring my eyes, torn between wishing her suffering would end and dreading the day it finally would.

Her voice visits me in dreams, and her presence startles me in the quiet, like a shadow moving in familiar light. I still hear her sometimes. Even after death, her voice returns in fragments—"I love you" in English, other times as a sudden swell of presence in my mind.

I don't go to her grave. I couldn't even approach her coffin at the funeral to place a flower on it. Facing the grave would make it final, and I still might not be ready. But I believe she's with me, and for now, that's enough.

Even so, there were moments of close-

9—THE INHERITANCE

ness at the end. She spoke more openly with my sister Elva, and I held onto that with gratitude. Those years, though heavy and uneven, carved out a deeper understanding of her and of myself.

But not all closeness extended beyond her. When she died, my siblings and I grieved apart. We didn't gather to name our pain or trade memories aloud. We slipped back into our own lives, carrying loss like separate vessels. Only through writing have I poured out what I carried, though I cannot speak for them. I often wonder what it would have been like if we had spoken more, admitting how frightened we were, how much we held in. Yet even in silence, I think we understood.

For me, time slowed. The rush fell away, and I let myself sit inside the grief instead of running from it. For the first time, I rested without guilt. In that stillness, something softened. I no longer held only her sorrow. I held her love, her memory, her quiet strength.

Through her decline, I also began to see

my father differently. For so long, I had stared only at the sharp edges—his anger, his drinking, his cruelty. I hadn't wanted to acknowledge the wounds beneath, didn't know how. But grief forced me to turn the stone over. I began to see that everyone in our family had been braving the storm in their own way, myself included.

As Gabor Maté explains in *In the Realm of Hungry Ghosts*, the limits we live with are rarely random—they take root in childhood and grow across generations, passed down like heirlooms no one meant to hold onto.

I began to wonder if the way I looked at my father—with disappointment, confusion, and longing—was the same way my own son once looked at me. That thought loosened something in me, not to excuse the past, but to see it with sharper eyes. I may never know the exact shape of my son's feelings, but I understand the ache of distance.

Pain runs through families like water seeping through cracks, finding its way into each generation unless someone decides to

9—THE INHERITANCE

seal the leak. I am still in that work—not to rewrite past chapters, but to imagine a future untethered to the familiar, unhealthy patterns of years past.

My father's body has slowed in old age, but his gaze is still sharp, his voice still a command in the room. I once thought grief might have softened him, but it hasn't. He carries on as though change were never part of his vocabulary. When I visit, I listen for the turn in the conversation. If it bends toward bitterness, I steer it gently away. That's my signal to leave. I no longer stay out of duty. I stay only while it feels respectful—to him, and to myself.

Lilia left, Elva, Mom, Ernie, Carlos, Me 1990's

I am still learning how to live in my mother's absence. I sit at my desk and look at her photo. I grieve every day. But I also do what she couldn't. I say yes to what she would have feared. I listen to my voice instead of silencing it. She didn't believe freedom was possible. I do.

GRIPPED

Her death didn't draw a line; it rewove the fabric of my life. What she left behind is stitched now into love, memory, and strength. I no longer carry only her silence. I also carry her story, and because of that, I move through the world differently.

10—TURNING THE PAGE

I've come to see change as less about repair work and more like stepping into a room I once locked myself out of. For years, I believed freedom meant sealing every crack, mending every wound, and perfecting every flaw. Now I know better. I'm no longer standing in the doorway waiting for a better version of myself to appear. I am already here, in this body, speaking with this voice, at this moment. I refuse to shrink down or believe fear is something I just have to live with.

I'm still sorting through my thoughts, reflecting, and learning how to stand fully in my own life. But I no longer carry burdens that were never mine. I'm no longer trapped in the same storyline, acting out the same scenes. I've chosen forgiveness, for others and for myself. In that choice, I've found a steadiness.

My grandson's patience remains vivid in my memory. At eighteen, he carried a kind of wisdom I hadn't expected. During one of the darkest stretches of my life, he stood beside me—quiet, steady, unshaken. He didn't try to fix anything. He simply anchored me with his presence. That, to me, is love.

When my son walked away, I eventually believed he was protecting himself. During the first season of my podcast, the seventh episode I recorded, "Echoes of Silence," addressed our estrangement, and it took several attempts before I could finish it without breaking down. Speaking those words aloud helped me express the ache and made me hope that someone listening might feel less alone.

I poured myself into work, applying

everything I had learned in order to help others find their own way through pain. Choosing to mend myself wasn't a single act. It was a decision I made again and again, even on the days when it felt like dragging a weight uphill. I told myself that if my son had found peace and never spoke to me again that I could learn to live with that.

Then one day, the phone rang.

It was him. He said his fiancée was on speakerphone, and the children were with him. He asked if I wanted to help watch them. Though my voice stayed even, my heart thudded like a drum against my ribs. "Yes, Mijo," I said softly, "I would love to help." His fiancée then asked me to save the date for their wedding. I was flooded with excitement.

I had met her once before at my oldest granddaughter's softball game. She carried herself with a quiet energy that drew me in, like a light you notice without trying. She acknowledged me with respect and without judgment, her warmth unmistakable. There was a steadiness in her presence that felt rare, and I understood right away why she mattered to my son. Hearing her voice on the phone that day only deepened that impression, and I felt a spark of hope rush through me.

When I arrived at his house to visit my grandchildren, I immediately sensed a calm in my son that hadn't been there before. He moved with an ease that felt unfamiliar; his voice carried an even cadence, and his gestures were measured. As he showed me through the rooms, I found myself listening more to the music of his tone rather than to the words themselves. When I looked into his eyes, the guardedness I once knew was gone, something steadier—peace—finally settling in him.

At the wedding, I didn't need to be at the center to feel connected. Watching him and his bride laugh and dance with my grandchildren was enough—it was beautiful, complete in its own way. What stayed with me was the realization that their lives are theirs to shape. I had my season to raise a family. Now my role is different: I support from the edges, cheer from the sidelines, and love without needing to lead.

My relationship with my son no longer lives only in the past. We've both changed, and though our conversations may be few, they feel lighter, more honest. I don't know what the future will hold, but I sense a mutual respect that wasn't there before. I see him as a man traveling his own path. We're not rehashing past traumas; instead, we're allowing space for something new, something more genuine.

I've found a softer kind of peace within myself now. Some days, the past still bangs on the door, louder than I'd like, but I don't let it take the lead anymore. I meet the hard moments directly, speak with clarity, and no longer wound others just to shield myself. I've also stopped swallowing my words to keep the air calm. I acknowledge what once was and set it back down where it belongs.

My marriage has changed, too. It isn't flawless, but it's more honest. We give each other room to stand as we are. We've learned to listen differently. Letting go of the urge to reshape him has altered our relationship with each other. I take more time before speaking, voice what I need without sharpening it, and keep myself from taking every word to heart. As we grow older, we do so with more awareness, and that matters to me.

I've made peace with the woman I used to be and with every version of myself before her: little Lourdes hiding under the bed, arms wrapped around her siblings while fear rattled her body; the teenager who wore armor just to get through the day; the young woman who worked tirelessly but doubted her worth; and the mother who longed to do better but didn't yet know how. They didn't have all the tools. Some were angry, tired, or worn thin, yet they kept moving forward. I no longer judge them. I carry them with me —not as weights to drag behind me, but as markers of where I've been.

There came a point when reflection wasn't enough. I needed to face the younger self I had left behind. In my mid-

10—TURNING THE PAGE

thirties, I closed my eyes, drew in a long breath, and let my mind travel back to find little Lourdes still crouched under the bed. In that moment, I imagined lifting her into my arms, holding her close, and whispering, "Aquí estoy contigo. No tengas miedo, mi amor. Nunca te voy a dejar." ("I am here with you. Don't be afraid, my love. I will never leave you.") Each time I return to that image, it moves something deep inside me, offering not repair for the past, but presence for the part of me that had been waiting the longest.

Little Lourdes still appears now and then. I don't push her away. She no longer has to vanish to make space for the woman I've become. Instead, I see her standing there, no longer hiding, simply smiling; she is calm, safe, and seen.

My writing has grown bolder, stripped of disguise and closer to the bone. Though I paused my podcast, *Growing Older Together,* in December 2024, it will return soon. I've built a business that reflects who I am now and gives me a voice I didn't always believe I deserved. Every so often, the past calls to me, but I don't fear it anymore. I don't need to retrace every step of who I've been, though sometimes I choose to. The difference now is that I know which parts are mine to carry and which I can finally set down.

    I no longer hold onto what isn't mine. I'm still learning, still becoming, but I'm honest with myself now, and that truth changes everything.

ACKNOWLEDGMENTS

To my parents, who showed me strength, and to my mom, who showed me resilience, perseverance, and love.

Lilia, Carlos, Elva, and Ernie—we lived through the same story, but each of us carried it in our own way. I am grateful for the respect you have always shown me as your older sister and for the comfort of knowing you were at my side.

Mijo, my son, you have been the one who taught me what no one else could. Your decision to walk away was an act of courage, and in choosing yourself, you gave me the chance to finally choose myself too.

Marisela, you have been like a sister to me. You handed me the key that opened the door to my childhood, and with it came the chance to face what I had locked away.

To my grandchildren, you are always in my heart. The love you've given me continues to remind me what it means to be held by family.

To my editor, Anaiah, you helped me bring out the parts of my story I once left in fragments, and your encouragement gave me the confidence to write what I had only carried inside.

And to my family and friends who gave me feedback on covers, titles, and drafts—thank you for taking the time to lend me your eyes and your honesty.

ABOUT THE AUTHOR

Lourdes Valtierra Dirden is drawn to the darker corners of the human experience, where truth lives just beneath the surface. A fan of psychological thrillers, crime, and horror, she enjoys podcasts like *Chilling Tales for Dark Nights*.

Her memoir *Gripped: The Weight I Refused to Carry* and her first book, *Going Solar: The Homeowner's Handbook*, reflect her range as a personal storyteller and nonfiction writer.

Through her business, currently rebranding from VA 4 Solutions, Lourdes collaborates with authors and professionals to develop content, design visuals, and manage the production of books, podcasts, and related media. She is also the founder of Think Books, an independent publishing imprint, and the host of the podcast *Growing Older Together*, now in its second season.

ABOUT THE EDITOR

Anaiah Davis is a first-generation college graduate with a Bachelor of Arts in English Creative Writing from Bradley University. She is a die-hard mystery fan, with a soft spot for romance, a deep love for young adult literature, and a growing admiration for poetry. Some of her all-time favorite fiction titles include *Small Great Things* by Jodi Picoult, *Beloved* by Toni Morrison, *A Good Girl's Guide to Murder* by Holly Jackson, *That's Not My Name* by Megan Lally, and *All Good People Here* by Ashley Flowers.

RESOURCES

BOOKS

Gabor Maté and Peter A. Levine Ph.D.
In the Realm of Hungry Ghosts: Close Encounters with Addiction (2010)
This book is for anyone who wants to understand trauma and childhood development, especially how early experiences shape behavior and family patterns.

John Bradshaw
Healing the Shame That Binds You (2005)
If you're looking to understand how shame shows up in families, where it comes from,

and how it affects the way we see ourselves, this is a book for you.

Marisa Peer
Tell Yourself a Better Lie: Use the power of Rapid Transformational Therapy to edit your story and rewrite your life (2022)
This book is for anyone who wants to better understand how self-talk shapes their life and how changing those internal stories can help shift patterns like low confidence, self-doubt, or disconnection from yourself.

Jim Kwik
Limitless Expanded Edition: Upgrade Your Brain, Learn Anything Faster, and Unlock Your Exceptional Life (2023)
If you want simple tools to help build better habits, think more clearly, and feel more confident, check out this book. It's for anyone looking to improve focus, memory, and learn how to break limiting beliefs.

NOTE: Gabor Maté and Marisa Peer have appeared together in online events like

RESOURCES

Healing Days in September 2025, where they shared their expertise on trauma, healing, and the subconscious mind.

FITNESS & MINDSET

Dave Durell, Strength After 50, https://www.strengthafter50.com/
I had been following Dave's emails and posts for a few years before reaching out to train with him online in January 2025, during my mom's final months. He was easy to talk to and attentive. He watched my form on the deadlift and dumbbell row. It was the first time working with a trainer online, and I loved it. He followed up after the session and sent extra resources without being asked. Even after I paused my training about two weeks after the session, his emails continued to remind me what my body needed, and why it mattered to return to it. We've recently reconnected via email, and I've started training again.

RESOURCES

Susan Niebergall Fitness, https://susanniebergallfitness.com/
Susan was one of the first trainers I followed when I got serious about powerlifting. She's a year older than me and focuses on strength training for older adults. Her Instagram posts are both informative and encouraging, often showing simple ways to modify exercises and make them more accessible.

Elizabeth Valdez, Heartfelt Wellness Hypnosis, https://heartfeltwellnesshypnosis.com/
Elizabeth combines formal RTT (Rapid Transformation Therapy) training from Marisa Peer with a grounded, personal approach. The custom recording she created for me became a quiet part of my healing. Our follow-ups helped me notice changes I might've dismissed—less tension, fewer critical thoughts, and more room for reflection. Her work helped me track progress I wasn't used to recognizing.

RESOURCES

BUSINESS & PRODUCTIVITY

Billie Gardner, Desire to Done (VA Introvert Club), https://desiretodone.com/
I found Billie through her podcast. She offered practical advice tailored for introverts who were virtual assistants, without the usual hustle-driven pressure. When I joined her VA Club, I found more than guidance, I found a community of VA's who treated me like kin. The tools and support matched the pace and mindset I needed to grow my business.

www.ingramcontent.com/pod-product-compliance
Lightning Source LLC
Chambersburg PA
CBHW030556080526
44585CB00012B/399